Jim Dunn

SPUYTEN DUYVIL
New York City

ISBN 978-1-956005-56-1
Cover Photo: Jim Dunn, "Rafe's Chasm" January, 2021

Library of Congress Cataloging-in-Publication Data

Names: Dunn, Jim, 1963- author.
Title: This silence is a junkyard / Jim Dunn.
Description: New York City : Spuyten Duyvil, [2022]
Identifiers: LCCN 2022012899 | ISBN 9781956005561 (paperbac
Subjects: LCGFT: Poetry.
Classification: LCC PS3604.U559 T48 2022 | DDC 811/.6--dc23
LC record available at https://lccn.loc.gov/2022012899

MOMENTS OF UNITY
BEGOTTEN BY CHAOS

Jim Dunn's poetry belongs as much to those strange and unplumbed dream regions of a Robert William's painting, as they do to the brawny armed world of Whitman's men and women. Truth be told, both of these worlds; the surreal psychoscape and the old elemental Earth, make up a unifying essence, whether we accept the contradiction or not.

Jim's attention and that of these poems is placed on a new way of hearing old tunes, walking within Thoreau's 20 acres, or reckoning the ancient ocean. If poets are of any use they make a practice of this, allowing their imagination to re-see and return to an ever changing world despite the obstinate ignorance promulgated by our still largely Puritan society. I say Puritan for, with the exception of a few excursions to northern California in search of Jack Micheline and any other remnants of indefatigable beatitude, the spirit of place in these poems is one of Hawthornes' *The Scarlet Letter*; Salem, Beverly, Gloucester, Boston, the Eastern Seaboard, roughly 300 years later.

With *This Silence is a Junkyard*, Jim Dunn has offered us a glimpse of his devotion to what his dear friend, Gerrit Lansing, calls "balling rondures" and "droopy streets" reminding us that we still can access our own newness and giving us a sense of what it truly means to be back in your own backyard. This space is not dominated by materialism, but rather, as Jim shows with brevity and grace, is a realm of the freely spiritual.

These gnomic poems will certainly arouse whoever they encounter to take notice of those minute particulars that make up our world and thereby perceive Whitman's cosmic, yet common vision. Having been a friend of this man, on the road and here on Cape Ann, I've felt that I was with someone akin to Peter Falk, (a man Jim met in Philadelphia as a boy on location of Elaine May's chaotic *Mickey and Nicky* (1976)) who in *Wing's of Desire* (1987) encourages his compañero Bruno Ganz to leave his life of exclusivity as an angel and embrace the transitory, at times heart breaking procession of life and death here on Earth, if only for a moment of love.

Gabriel Barboza
Gloucester, MA
February 2022

Silence is a Junkyard

Tall reeds in the Fenway
bob their heads into the wind
strange men on my trail

This silence is a junkyard
guarded by angry pit bulls
with razor sharp teeth

The Franklin Zoo ape
holds the sadness of the world
within her dark eyes

Empire state building
outside my kitchen window
fingering the sky

Winter white silence,
after the storm, broken by
scraping of shovels

The ghosts in your skeleton

dance on puppet strings

controlled by the wind

lightning flashes night
an obscene glimpse of the trees
crying for the rain

in these tricky times

there is a thin smoky veil

between fate and fatal

Driving fast and buzzed
through fields of sprouting houses
where farmland once was.

Frail cat in my lap
droops slowly into deep sleep
with one paw outstretched

Silence—my defense;
closets in my skeleton
locked from the inside

The ocean and time
advance inevitably
The jetty stands defiant

Winter sky looks bruised
sunset over New Jersey
sea swallows light

Christmas eve alone,
bow of sunken concrete ship
in the wind-whipped sea

Night brings out the stars
The wind whispers through the
trees
You, here with me now

Dylan at Newport

riding bikes through the mansions

Ain't goin' nowhere

Full of vicodin

After surgery on my head

Found the ether dome

the sound of hard rain

falling from broken gutters

a mad waterfall

Leaves fall sad yellow
naked trees stand shivering
in the raping wind

A single star fell
After Thanksgiving dinner
November by night

took two painkillers
in the aimless afternoon
New York City Rain

buildings dissappear

into the clouds descending

like visions erased.

Silence is broken
a morning motorcycle
gunning for the dawn

The breath of linemen
swirls in puffs majestically
furious horses

Snow flakes and blue smoke
mingle with violin sounds
cold November night

moths drunk on the night

wrestle themselves in morning

heavy with the light

Snow falls quietly
On the winter wind that blows
Down this city street

April rain reflects
the early morning street lights
in puddled mirrors

Coach tells her swimmer
Go and be the synchronized
Sorceress of the wind

Loud noise is my friend

True silence my master

Dogs barking know both

catching a quick glimpse
of Salem Harbor at dawn
from the morning train

The Autumn sun sets

winking goodbye to two boys

swimming on the roof

Pale morning light creeps
through the darkened trees as the
dog takes his first piss

The wind marches on
A Distant roar gathering
Lions of winter

Dog barks in the night
Sliding door left cracked open
The dawn is the thief.

Sweet morning silence
In the dusk before the dawn
Broken by the bells

As the chaos swirls
Uncertainty reigns supreme
Pursue and endure

Early morning freeze
Blue ice tongue licking the sky
Clean of morning stars

Early evening moon
Hangs faintly blue in the sky
A thumb print on glass

Dog of sad wrinkles
Stands on guard at the window
Waiting for some sign

From out of nowhere

A bundle of magic dropped

Into your life's lap

Dog waits to come in
Verdant leaves bob lazily
In the summer breeze

mountains in mirror
purple cattle in the sky
masspike moon hangs low

the afternoon sun

shines from the place where god lived

to where angels bathe

Keep a white sea shell
In the pocket of your heart
In case you need it

Count the tiny lights
It's impossible to know
who turned them on

Wanting only death
the old snapper turtle swims
toward the island

My pen conducting
angry clouds heavy with storms
broken by the sun

Three sexy peacocks
approach the smiling street
cops—
Halloween Parade

Song of the sparrows
above the coughing busses—
momentary grace

Putting on my socks
is sometimes the hardest thing
that I do all day

Sandy haired student
writing her secrets long hand
in suede leather pants

The old attendant
at the station in Big Sur
said, "I like your hat."

Dogs walk their masters
in the gravel of the dog park
in Washington Square

The sinister beauty

of the bell tower in Berkeley

that's a load of bricks

Death wears your church clothes,
on makeshift Sunday morning,
right down to the shoes

The summer heat rises
distorting the dancing road
that lies just ahead

The bread for the birds

scattered, covered and smothered

by the snow's blanket

The seven sisters
cross their legs dazzlingly
the stars go out for the night

The common rhythm
of human life is routine
punctuated by orgies

cat licks his silence
with a tick tock stop watch tongue
on soft fur of time

Walking through Walden
looking for the Thoreau House
Found a pile of rocks

A clue to your soul

Found within the flickering

Lost within the sun

dark clouds come early
on a humid summer night
lightning strikes the street

monkey on my car
pissing on the window-
Jersey safari

close to the shore

blue shark waits in the shadow

of the lifeguard's boat

fishing for the blues
humpback whale blows sea mist cloud
didn't catch many

the apocalypse

didn't stop me from drinkin'

in the tragic shadows

tourists are curious

to see where god stepped upon

the glorious ant hills

slept on my dad's roof

just to hear the cricket's roar

and trumpets of geese

beat up piano

in the same living room

I searched for easter eggs

Jamaican preacher

on the 9 train downtown

tells me what I know

drum case left alone
near the door unattended
let's sit somewhere else

from Hoboken shores

they are not there anymore

the city's ghost limbs

Chelsea boys stare us down
from the cafe viceroy tables
the war is downtown

Tiny river town

of canals and locomotives

and Washington's crossing

saw a guy I knew
hitchhiking towards the river—
couldn't stop in time

hawks drift like mad clouds

showing off their silouettes

against a harsh blue

threats of frost announced
afternoon shadows lengthen
wind is my master

Climbing the light house
young boy chirps like the State
bird
to hear his echo

Patience, a virtue—

Five boys on a dead end street

Raising holy hell

Remembering you—
Geese honk in the afternoon;
Beat their wings in prayer

Football on your lawn

Waving hi on your tractor

Zen and the art of mowing

Randomness of fate
Two neighbors waving good-bye
'Twas nice knowing you.

torrential downpours
disguised as gentle showers
please rinse off my brain

Crazy kids jumping
In the Arctic afternoon
On a trampoline

In the misty fog
Newport Bridge over the bay
A road to heaven

My dad closed his eyes
And said, "Jesus Fucking Christ!"
He knew he was dead

Snow finally melting
Dirty mountains of grey snow
Rivulets of tears

Cotton clouds unfurl

Like beautiful angels' breath

Fuming on the sky

The early dawn birds
Singing to the summer hum
In the rising sun

Sunday morning sun
Beautiful brilliant orange
I drive into it.

THE CHASM

BETWEEN THE FULL MOON
AND THE RISING SUN

Caught upon the rocks, a slippery place
Between the living moment and the dead dream
There lies behind me the nocturnal soul of
night's engine
Orchestrating the dance and the music of the
endless sea
Ahead the gulls bring news of the coming light
The clouds are set aflame from underneath by
the slightest touch
Of the fiery fingertips of the praying pointed
hands of a new day
First a blinking eye and then the blazing face of
ecstasy

Behind me the moon lowers its hollow shell upon
the trees lined against the sky
The clouds are fields of rolling joy from which rises
the royal white chariot
Led by glorious horses frozen in mid-gallop
Heroically stoic in their conquering charge over
immense distances
The copper shimmer of the wet rocks shines
between what is left of night and
What is to become of the day bathed in new light,
dressed in wild white flowers of the clouds
The foamy sea throwing her bouquet against the
silent rocks standing fast
Between the full moon and the rising sun.

FISHING AT THE MOUTH OF A CHASM

Casting a prayer into the sea
Standing upon the bare knuckles
     Of the holy coast
The sea breathes around me
Whispering her glorious secrets-
       There is ruthless danger in beauty
           And
       There is ruthless beauty in danger

I catch a blessing in
the foamy tide and throw it back
 into the sea
The sun cracks open
     The sky
And we are all doomed
     In the daylight.

RAFE'S CHASM

The sun is born an orange ball
and dies a hazy yellow flower

FOLDED SORROWS

For Bob

Spread out against the sky
They seem immense
A sky of blackbirds delivering
Their own version of an avian eclipse
Miles of beating wings
No measure: a circumference of infinity
There seems to be a secret door in this city
That opens downward like a trap door
To the bottom of an all encompassing
Disheartening sadness
A laundromat lost in time
That washes tears clean
Of their salty connection to the sea
Where warmly waits the folded sorrows
To be carried upstairs and put away.

SUNSPOTS AND SMOKE RINGS

In search of Katherine Lane Deems
      Chimney Estate
I happened upon a statuesque
      Deer standing frozen
      Beside the pylons
That forbid parking and sunbathing
On hidden treasured beaches

  The seventh wave on
The longest day will be a flattening
    Of the curve of love and
The splintering plank of hate.

I am the fire. I hear it in
My ears. I throw myself
Into my work. I sound it out.

A crackling of the soul
That burns from the inside out.
Sunspots and smoke rings
I appear to be.

POWER WASH THE SOULS

For Ivan, Mandy & Greg

Ivan loved to
power wash everything
Greg proclaimed at his
Australian funeral
A lobsterman gone
Out to sea
To power wash
The stars.

I rid the deck of dark &
dirty secrets

      with jets of holy water
water that does not replenish
water that removes

any trace of

time & buildup

I power wash the souls

    of lonely porches

        removing lichen, mold & moss

with the laser focus

of mindful water

    that cannot be imbibed

    that cannot bless

        but works wonders

            like an aqua-velvet

charm.

6/6/9

For we have travelled
far along the harbor
upon vessels
unburdened & free

To visit unannounced
the silent spirits
of afternoon rooms

Two boys and one man
with diminishing vision
(Triton riders and the lonely man
from Atlantis City)
stopped by

        to conjure up

        drifting mysteries

at the very least

to skip these memories eternally

on the serene surface

of the setting sea

6/6/10

Through the window as dreams go
I spy you snowy white on the couch
Koko roams free sniffing furiously
On the trail of Hector who left the
Remains of bird in the hallway not
As a gift but more as an offering
in a beautiful primitive way.

Out into the new light of morning
Of East Gloucester past Ferrini's frame house
And Charlie Olson's Carpentry shop
Snaking around Niles beach
Where Willie Alexander's great dream
Of Olson's duel of words with Ferrini took place
Now an immortalized mural
On a Beverly parking lot wall

Walking through the Relic Sandplain Grassland
The rare Open Heath Seine field
A field about nothing but nets
Where generations of Seine fisherman
Laid them out upon the grass
To catch nothing but slowly repair and
Dry the netting upon the arid sandy soil.
Along the path, wheeling slowly in the dry dirt
A dusty snapper turtle buries her eggs
In the sandy solitude.

Koko pants and pulls, pulls and pants
Purple tongue hanging out of his considerable
        snout
A majestic manatee with the wrinkles of Old
        Chinese wisdom
He picks up a tick on each shoulder
Stealth black badges of roaming free

Walking with wings on our feet
Guarded by the golden chariot
Of the lost sleeping lion
Roiling like ocean clouds
Toward the future thunder of
Your harbor home.

You walk with the gait of a gardener
Open and true.
Your breathing is freer
Your heart keeps time unconfined
Free to roam through unchecked clocks
And stopped watches dusted with stillness

Yankee Division Highway
6/6/19

In defense of the depth charge frogman
Diving deeper to wire the water to explode

The day starts as an ocean
And ends as a star
Waves of water and bands of light
Wash over the hours and shine the night

We are almost there
if the rest stop is home (it is)
I celebrate the Beverly Rest Area
The only respite on the
Yankee Division Highway
Where Giles Corey took his
Shortcut through the Witches Woods
He made such great time

From Salem to Gloucester

That it had to be sorcery

And not a sensible route through the woods

The shortcut proved he was a warlock

And when they heaved boulders upon his chest

To coax a confession from his pressed lips

His only response was "More weight."

And more weight was applied and

Crushed Giles to death but his spirit

Still lingers just beyond the rest stop

Off Common Lane in the Witches Woods

The winter wind as it passes through the trees

Whispers "More weight"

The trucks at the rest stop idle with

Running lights aglow humming

A diesel tune for the Cape Ann Boulders

That labored his breath as it

Whistled away from his last words.

6.6.21

A day the heat
Was on
Couldn't
Fish with a broken pole
I was drawn to the chasm anyway
Cassandra's sweet song
Was dancing in the air

The fox kits have gone
Left their drainpipe home
For the wilds of Coolidge
Point
The grass waves silently
In their absence
I am gone too left alone
To my own obsessions

Running away from the
Rolling boulders of my troubles
Lost on the way and muted
Even as I talk loudly to myself
Muted in my soul
Gerrit's advice on his deathbed
Rings true again like
A morning Church goer's secret bell
"You're too hasty!"

My crackling electric live wire
Moves me in fast motion
My tongue runs after my mind
Hitting glossalalia speed bumps
I must slow down to speed up
The process.
Walk with a sailor's gait
On Crane's Beach-

The windmills of Gloucester

Whirl on the horizon

Creating their own frenetic energy

To share with the people of Polis

A dip in the ocean is a dry run

For the baptism of my

Glorious ghosts.

GHOUCESTER, MA

Granite glistens in the golden glaze of receding tide
These rocks are slick reminders
of how easily it all slips away
They are unmoved by daytime and drama
Of the pleading sea
Pleading to see the spectres dressed in the
Morning garb of birds in flight standing and praying
Some swooping and cursing
Dip dive and pedal your desire
For want of a better word
For want of a bitter sword
The Cut cuts both ways
Why cross out when you can cross over?
A myriad of mirrors
Pick your reflection carefully
Left-handed left holding

Right minded right here

They are the mist, the steam, the haze

They are the sea spray, the rain remnant, the
dew

They are condensation, the beads of sweat, the
tears

St Peter's feast of the fiesta, fisher of men,
clammer of souls

Statues are crying, buildings are confused

Carry your patron saint under your eyelids

To flash a sign of the cross when you roll your
eyes

West Meets east in the middle of the harbor

Paint factory pain points abandoned boats
abandoned hopes

There is nothing worse than seeing nothing
there

But swearing the nothing you saw is a

lighthouse of memories

Lit up with the rotating eye of blinking experience

Ghoucester MA harbors ghost ships invisible deck

hands and men reduced to

A name on their minds floating like a golden

thought of forgiveness

to a deserving beach crowd watching the whale.

Acknowledgments

Many thanks and eternal gratitude to the editors of the small press journals where some of these poems have appeared:

Micah Ballard and Garrett Caples (Skeletor and He-Man) at *Castle Grayskull: a magazine of 'verse*

Jim Behrle at *Can We Have Our Ball Back?*

Tamas Panitz, Whit Griffin, Chloe Bliss Snyder and Carlos Lara at *Blazing Stadium*

I dedicate this book to my friend and musician, Ash Bowie. Many poems in this book were written as a spontaneous addendum to our long and sustained correspondence—we continued a dialogue over many years, trading short poems back and forth; his attention and care inspired a good portion of this book. I can't thank him enough for his friendship and inspiration over the years.

Big love and special thanks to Angela, Seamus, and Gavin Dunn for their love and unconditional support.

Eternal thanks to my friend and comrade in poetry, Gabe Barboza, who truly listens and who took these poems to heart.

Many thanks and appreciation (in random order) to the community of family, friends, poets, artists and musicians who friendship and work inspire me to keep on keepin' on: Ammiel Alcalay, Joe Torra, Jim Behrle, Erik Lomen, John Giglio, Fanny Howe, Christina Davis, Ruth Lepson, Rosemary, Michael Franco, Amanda and James Cook, Greg Cook, Patrick Doud, Michael Bronski, Dan Bouchard, Andrew Peterson, Micah Ballard, Sunnylyn Thibodeaux, Lorca Ballard, Derek Fenner, Garrett Caples, Ryan Gallagher, Duncan McNaughton, Mary Lou Lord, Raymond Foye, Seth Stewart, Robbie Dewhurst, Carol Weston, John Galloway, Anna Salamone, Timotha Doane, Mitch Manning, John Mulrooney, Rachel Layne, Linda Norton, David Abel, Henry Ferrini, Bing McGilvray,

Ben Mazer, Kevin Gallagher, Colleen Michaels, Willie Alexander, April Ridge, Lee Zeoli, Fred Gianelli, Joe Shepard, Mike Flynn, Dan Bacon, David Amram, Meg Smith, Frank Spignese and the Spignese family, John and Gina Preziosa, Clifford Condon, Dr. Joe Venneri, Jeffrey Todd Dunn, Thomas Michael Dunn, Gregory Scott Dunn and Joan Curran. A special thanks to Neeli Cherkovski (and Jessie and Orion as well) for his poetry, friendship, and for his advice in getting this book into the world.

And to Tod Thilleman and Aurelia at Spuyten Duyvil; thank you for your patience and support in making this book a reality.

And finally, a heartfelt thanks and glance back towards those friends and family gone but whose spirits shine forth from the pages of this book: Bill Corbett, Kevin Dunn, Big Jim Dunn, Gerrit Lansing, Jack McCarthy, Charley Shively, Jack Powers, Margo Lockwood, Aldo Tambellini, and John Wieners.

JIM DUNN is the author of *Soft Launch* (Bootstrap Press/Pressed Wafer, 2008), *Convenient Hole* (Pressed Wafer, 2004), and *Insects In Sex* (Fallen Angel Press, 1995). His work has appeared in *Castle Grayskull, Blazing Stadium, Can We Have Our Ball Back?, Bright Pink Mosquito, The Process, eoagh, Gerry Mulligan, Cafe Review, Meanie*, and the anthology in tribute to John Wieners, *The Blind See Only In This World*. He edited the John Wieners Journal, *A New Book From Rome* with Derek Fenner and Ryan Gallagher of Bootstrap Press.